BEAUTIFUL TRAGEDIES III

A HellBound Books Publishing LLC Book
Houston TX

A HellBound Books LLC Publication
Copyright © 2023 by HellBound Books Publishing LLC
All Rights Reserved

Cover and art design by
HellBound Books Publishing LLC

No part of this book may be reproduced, stored in a retrieval system, or transmitted by any means, electronic, mechanical, photocopying, recording or otherwise without written permission from the author
This book is a work of fiction. Names, characters, places and incidents are entirely fictitious or are used fictitiously and any resemblance to actual persons, living or dead, events or locales is purely coincidental.

www.hellboundbookspublishing.com

INTRODUCTION:

Love can be an overwhelming feeling and oftentimes indescribable. But love isn't always about the butterflies in the stomach when you first kiss or stolen glances that cause your heart to race. Sometimes it can be ugly and dreadful. It can lead to shattered hearts, melancholic souls, and tear-stained pillows. In some cases, it can even lead to murderous thoughts…and questionable and frightful actions.

Beauty and tragedy – this poetry anthology blurs the lines that divide the two.

There's true passion behind the words written within these pages from over forty talented poets. The poets bring quite a variety of dark poetry to the table, all organized and edited by HellBound Books' own Dark Poet Princess, Xtina Marie. As a reader, you can expect varied lengths, different tones, and a wide range of stories all skillfully told through bewitching and tragic poetry.

This assortment of poetry from such an array of voices is truly a unique reading experience. After you finish reading Beautiful Tragedies 3, you'll be hungry for more. I hope you devour the work of all the poets within this beautifully macabre anthology.

-Brianna Malotke,
author of Don't Cry on Cashmere and
Fashion Trends, Deadly Ends

CONTENTS:

Xtina Marie
A Burning House
Cowering in the Chaos
With Scarred and Damaged Arms
Wildfire
I'm Sinking

M Ennenbach
collected desires
i dream of you and wake to a world of painful longing
tinder to her inferno
nights like tonight

Gerri R. Gray
Not Quite a Sonnet
Maladjusted
Apathetically Yours
Strange Sorcery
Beneath a Cloud-Riddled Sky
Damaged

Yuan Changming
Tender in Between
Cherry Flowers
Do U Hear It?
Again, Looking Forward,
Etymology of Family: a Bilinguacultural Poem
Love Lost & Regained: for Li Lan

Marissa Garofalo
How Could You
Worthless
Darkest Hour
Fading
Dead Planet
Just a Girl
Her

LindaAnn LoSchiavo

Annabel Lee Breaks Her Silence by the Sea
   John A. Taylor
A Kiss in the Dark
Sustenance
The Lady Across the Meadow
   Bill Evans
Home at Last
Not Going Home
Betrayed
Power
Lilith
   Chris McAuley
Inner Demons
On a Knife Edge
The Voice of Creation
The Turning Key in My Mind
Anger
   T.L. Barrett
The Swinger's Lament
   Ed Ahern
The Woman in Question
   Veronica Kegel-Giglio
Story of Moira
We Made a Forever Pact
Her Greatest Love
He Told ME To Do It
I am the Doll that Watches out for Her
Lovely Lady in the Window
Lover Doll
The Quest for Love
   Brianna Malotke
Bespell My Heart
Decaying Heartache
Latest Home Renovation
   C.M. Godbout
Ghost

Karen Demmans
After You Died
Ripped
Tattoo
Wyd
Sarah Kay Collie
Come With Me
Wash me
My Soul
Victor Marrow
It Waves at You
Hansen Tor Adcock
Blue + Green = Red
Alexander Etheridge
Introspection
Winter Nightmare
Shawna Renée Lewis
Patchwork
Max Bindi
Dark Ballad of lost love
Gerardo Serrano R
The Downfall
Serena Daniels
Everything for Nothing
Josh Darling
All Choked Up
Jack the Ripper
You're Going to Die Taking a Shit
Aurynanya
A Meal of You
In Between
One of Them
Soul Searching
The Host
Christopher T. Dabrowski
The Reflection

Ravenna Blazecroft
By Blasphemy Unbound
Megan Diedericks
The Rage Burns Red
Wanting
Travis J. Black
My Love is a Chimera
Denise Jury
Begging
Hurt
Story
Relocated
Samantha Hawkins
Shatter
A Candle Without a Flame
Margarita Glass
Keeping Score
Lexie Carver
Close Your Eyes
Home
Mine
Carlton Herzog
The Weeping Somnambulist
Thomas Stewart
The Long Defeat
Naomi Simone Borwein
Happy Birthday, on the anniversary of your death
Sofia Lago
Lady Midday
Kevin Hollaway
Lily and Me
Tom Duke
Thomasina's Momentous Day
Ana Cordoba
Dark Kinship
Katie Steffens

Blood on the Roses
Raindrops
Tonight, I hope I dream of fire
   Aurora Starr
Just Listen
I Won't Be There
The Perfect Lie
   Theresa Scott-Matthews
Eternal Garden
   KH
Lithium
Daddy's Little Crazy Monster
   Alan Meyrowitz
The Note
   Korbin Elsmore
Never Enough
The End
Lonely Nights
Alcoholism
   Rachel Morin
Sacred Sol
   Melysza Jackson
Bound
Drowning Sin
Fragile
   Hannah Faith
Stalker
Cuts and Bruises

A BURNING HOUSE
Xtina Marie

I used to
live in a
burning house,
watching
the fire
crawl up the
curtains
with every
bitter,
vile word
you spoke

each breath
I took
labored and
painful as I
inhaled the smoke
and lies
you served
daily with your
morning coffee,
a smile on your
deceitful lips
as you passed
the sugar bowl
laced with poison

I turned
a blind eye
as my skin blistered…

as it bubbled
and blackened,
the acrid smell
hanging horribly
in the air
after each
long night
alone in a
bed for two

I ignored
the appendages
that turned
to ash,
falling soundlessly
to the ground
until I tried
to escape
but there was
no longer
legs in which
to escape with
just a pile
of smoldering remains

The flames
consumed
and yet
I sat next
to you
while we ate
our dinner
in the
deafening
solitude
together

but alone
and I

watched

as we burned

COWERING IN THE CHAOS
Xtina Marie

you were a
a beach house
in a hurricane--
all pretty
decorations
and sharp edges…
as long as
I kept
the candles
stocked
and battened
down the
hatches,
I'd be safe
from the
impending
storm

but I
was never
that prepared,
and cowered
in the chaos
—powerless—
the only
sounds audible
were the howling
of the wind
and the steady
drum of rain
as they

beat upon
the walls with
undisguised rage
and fury

every storm
I'd tell myself
this time
I'd be ready
this time
will be
different
this time
I'd be equipped…

until
I was again

cowering
in the chaos

that
was
you

WITH SCARRED AND DAMAGED ARMS
Xtina Marie

The scars
decorating
her arms
are proof
she's still here
another day

despite
the mental
torment
constantly
plaguing her

whispering to her
she'll never
be good enough

never make a
difference

never amount to
anything

she no longer
believes
differently

it's her truth
and she's tired
of fighting
the overpowering

oppressive
thoughts
that scream
her insecurities

they know her
they love her
they embrace her

with scarred
and damaged arms

WILDFIRE
Xtina Marie

she's like
a wildfire
all hot and chaotic
and burning
everything
in her wake
despite
heroic efforts
to thwart
the destruction

                                              no one can tame
                                                    DISASTER

I'M SINKING
Xtina Marie

A melancholic
sadness
lives
inside me

a deep
fear
I'll always
have

lost
in my own
creation

I'm sinking

COLLECTED DESIRES
M Ennenbach

each morning
i sit with
coffee steaming
as the sparrows
hop excitedly
on the deck
awaiting the
monomolecular
edge of the
scalpel to open
a fresh wound
releasing a
flood of ink
in rancid decline
to pour across
cerulean lies
snapshots of a
shattered soul
refracting the
light she used
to shine so freely
now nothing more
than figments in
shadowed repose
pasting scabs
to tattered pages
chasing ghosts
as the razor
gleams in the
sunlight dancing
in tiny black eyes

wondering if today
the words will
find a safe harbor
from the tempest
raging in my
hollowed out skull
another offering
perchance to please
the heaven in
her crooked smile

collected desires.

I DREAM OF YOU AND WAKE TO A WORLD OF PAINFUL LONGING
M Ennenbach

everything seems
so overwhelmingly
everythingish
all of the
goddamned time
without ever seeming
to take a fucking break
untiredly spinning
miseries around
waning solar impudance
a constant pummeling
punctuated by
a miserable silence
where only the
consistent tinnitus
is the lullabye
for a fool filled
with scars in the
shape of smiles all
along his cardial nerve
i can close my eyes
and feel her pulled
tight against my chest
forming a circuit
where this overabundance
of hyperbolic adoration
can flow like a surge
of voltage going to
the only home it ever
longed for in her

perfectly pulsing heart

i dream of you and wake to a world of painful longing.

TINDER TO HER INFERNO
M Ennenbach

i never
feared her flame
no
i longed to
feed it
to let her
set the horizon
on fire
with her
beauty
like a thousand
fucking suns.
i knew
all that would
remain of my
loving remains
was a fool
burnt into
the side of
the building
with a sliver
in the shape
of her smile
where my
heart always
belonged.

tinder to her inferno.

NIGHTS LIKE TONIGHT
M Ennenbach

i wonder
on nights when
the ache is
all consuming
will it ever
fucking end?
worse though
i fear its
absence.
because
on most nights
the aching
is all there is.
patience
isn't something
i was born with
it was acquired
through pain.
now i cannot
seem to tell
if it is patience
or stubborn
perseverance
keeping me
consistently
aching so.
either way
it fucking sucks.

nights like tonight.

NOT QUITE A SONNET
Gerri R. Gray

Once upon a time you read my poems,
You found them too bleak, too dark,
and too weird,
The words that I penned you called depressing,
You said that I should write things
not so queer.

My desolation you found disturbing,
Cursing my verses you called sad bouquets,
You shredded the only thing that I loved.
How do I hate me? Let me count the ways.

I tried to light candles in my darkness
But all that glimmered was self-denying.
My inner pain you never understood,
The more that I smiled, the more I felt like
dying.

MALADJUSTED
Gerri R. Gray

Always with a sneer
you called me a freak,
a misfit, a thing,
not worthy of love
and I believed
in my heart
that was true.
You made me hate
every bit of myself
almost as much
as you made me hate you.

How I remember
the times when you stated
you wished
I'd never been born.
I wished for that too,
so many, many times
and in my dark nights
I still do.

You never once said
that you loved me;
I wouldn't have believed you
even if you had.

And from your grim lips
there never came smiles
except when your words
would cut me so bad
I'd yearn to melt into

a royal blue dream,
from which I would
never return.

I cannot recall
if in spring or in summer
or fall you did leave.
The sun was shining,
your face was contorted
in one final sneer,
I remember it clearly.

Slowly the days
passed by into months,
and months passed by
into years
and then decades.
Never again did I see you
except
in my recurring nightmares
murdering me.

I heard you grew old
and sick, then you died.
I thought that I should
have felt something
within me,
anything, one thing,
gladness or sadness.
But I felt nothingness,
emptiness,
numb.

Two thousand miles
I had put between us
but that, and a lifetime,

were never enough
to silence your voice,
that cruel, mocking voice,
from again and again
being heard,
or to make me forget
the pain
you inflicted,
the wounds that bleed
not with blood..

For inside my head
embedded are your words
like shrapnel
still cutting me
always so deep,
so viciously deep.

APATHETICALLY YOURS
Gerri R. Gray

I gave to you my heart in words,
inscribed on secret bits and pieces,
consonants and vowels unveiled
like ribbon-wrapped confessions.

Between your fingertips you crushed
each one until they turned to dust,
and then into the vicious wind
you cast them out like demons.

I wept your name, I cried, I cursed,
but all the while you looked away
and gazed upon a distant star
that matched your cold indifference.

You told me once, I love you too –
a love that filled my soul with winter.
Teardrops fell and turned to dew
that clung to morning petals.

STRANGE SORCERY
Gerri R. Gray

If, by some strange sorcery,
I could travel back in time
and make you look through
my eyes, perhaps you'd see
the monster I so despised,
and then perhaps you'd know
what it once felt like to feel,
or to wish that you couldn't
for the pain was so intense.

If, by some strange sorcery,
I could bring you back from
Hell, I'd gouge out your eyes
so you could never watch me
cry. I'd slice off your tongue
with your sharp x-acto knife
so you could never again
wound me with words that
burned like acid.

If, by some strange sorcery,
I could make you understand
I never wanted to hate you
or wish for you to die
but you gave me
no choice, you
bastard.

BENEATH A CLOUD-RIDDLED SKY
Gerri R. Gray

I followed you into the northern wood,
far from the glade where the pastel
songbirds played their summertime
tunes, and where dragonflies kissed
the tips of my fingers with fragile
caresses that felt like silk.

Exchanging soft cushions of green
for the stinging of nettles and the
snapping of twigs, I followed as
leafless, skeletal hands clawed at
my arms. The black-feathered
crows looked down from above
and offered their cackles like dirges.

The warmth of the sun turned to
chill as the trail ceased to be, and
your darkening shadow ceased
to care. I begged to turn back,
to run, but you said not to fear,
that I wasn't alone.

And out from the nowhere a wisp of
laughter drifted, soft like the sigh of a
gentle season dying. Holding your hand,
looking into your eyes, at that moment
I never felt more alone.

How much farther, I asked, but there
only came silence like swords from
your lips, and to an outcropping of

rocks you pointed, upon which we
climbed. And the wind intoned like
a serpent hissing.

A sacrificial altar thirsting for blood
to fuel the evil of its necromancy.
I stared up into the cloud-riddled
sky and imagined what flowers felt
when they died.

I felt your fingers upon my wrists, a
chaos of storms, inseverable madness.
My thoughts, like ripples formed
when drowning. No longer human, a
jumbled mosaic.

At that moment I yearned to cry out,
to make my voice pierce the
smothering trees, so that every
living thing could hear, could know
my despair, and maybe no longer
I'd feel alone.

But I found my tongue frozen,
unable to wail, stifled by the chant
of a madwoman's spell.
The snows fell upon me, then
melted away, and around my body
vines grew green.
Soon I became a nameless
thing, not living, not dead,
but somewhere in between.

Don't cry, you said, for I am your
muse, and someday this moment

a poem will be. You smiled and
then silence engulfed the world.

In reticence we counted
the stars as they died,
you alongside me, and I
alone.

DAMAGED
Gerri R. Gray

Damaged like the cover of some old book
whose tattered yellowed pages come undone.
Screwed up like a mirror's cracked reflection...
Is that me, or is that somebody else?

Broken like the promise of a lover
withered like a flower in October.
Chipped around the edges just a little;
you'd never know unless you looked up close.

Twisted inside out until my brain screams
and poems ricochet inside my skull.
Fractured outside in and glued together;
off the deep end like a true romantic.

Madness turns the key that starts the engine;
Mercy Street I never ever did find.

TENDER IN BETWEEN: FOR HELENA QI HONG
Yuan Changming

As night
Falls
Can day
Catch it
From the other
Side of
This world?

Meanwhile
The broken heart
Is being
Caressed by
All the fingers
Of starlight
As tender as
Illuminating

CHERRY FLOWERS
Yuan Changming

Since the darkest moment of last winter
Every cherry tree has been looking
Forward to the apparition of full spring
Until each bud cannot wait any more
But eagerly wake itself up
In the wee hours of morning, hoping
To get the first sight of the season

Only after all their leaves have fallen
To the chilly ground
Might they understand
Their flowers were the spring per se

DO U HEAR IT?
Yuan Changming

From the heart of the Pacific
Far beyond the Pandemic

A Moby Dick is screaming
As if to keep its throat clear

Or it would be choked to
Death with parcels of plastics

AGAIN, LOOKING FORWARD
Yuan Changming

I am bidding time in darkness
I am bidding darkness in time, silently

Counting the stars high above the double-
Glazed skylight of my mind, waiting
For the day to break again with just another
Happy surprise popping up on the small screen
Such as a greeting from my lost first love
An acceptance email from a magazine editor
A report about the vaccine against the virus
A green color twinkling across American markets
A quiet morning on the Indian-Pakistan
Frontline, all among other little exciting
Possibilities while

Darkness is bidding me in time, &
      Time bidding me in darkness, silently

ETYMOLOGY OF FAMILY: A BILINGUACULTURAL POEM
Yuan Changming

In English, family is a word to say:
Father
And
Mother
I
Love
You

Where as in Chinese, 家 is
A pictograph offering
A shelter 宀
To or a big pig 豕

SIMPLIFICATION OF CHINESE CHARACTERS REVIEWED: A BILINGUACULTURAL POEM

Yuan Changming

1/
Is it a linguistic coincidence or undeclared prophesy?
But 60 years after Mao Zedong approved
The scheme for simplifying Chinese characters
We are now living in an open & reformed age, where

愛/ai/ [love] has become a feeling without a heart: 爱

親/qin/ [kinship] someone who is not to be seen: 亲

兒/er/ [son] a person without his own brain: 儿

鄉/xiang/ [village] a place where there's no male: 乡

廠/chang/ [factory] a building with nothing inside: 厂

産/chan/ [manufacture] a process without production: 产

雲/yun/ [cloud] a nimbus offering no rainfall : 云

開/kai/ [open] an action to break something doorless: 开

導/dao/ [lead] a guidance without the Way: 导

2/
More than half a century long after
The simplification of classic Chinese characters
& almost half a century well after
China opened its doors & began its reforms
To shake off its deformities or backwardnesses:

魔 /mo/ remains the same as 魔 [evil], so does

鬼 /gui/ as 鬼 [ghost], so does

偷 /tou/ as 偷[steal], so does
黑 /hei/ as [darkness], so does
贪 /tan/ as 贪[greed], so does
赌 /du/ as 赌[gamble], so does
毒 /du/ as 毒[poison], so does
贼 /zhei/ as 贼[thief], so does
骗 /pian/ exactly as 骗[cheat,], which remains
As unchangeable as Chinese per se, or does it not?

LOVE LOST & REGAINED: FOR LI LAN
Yuan Changming

1/ Love Lost: a Rambling Sentence
How I sometimes wonder
Whether it is because you wear
Your years so well or because the years
Wear you so well that I fell in mad love with
You after as long as 42 years of separation without
Knowing each other's whereabouts, again at first sight
With the whole Pacific Ocean between our shortening arms

2/ Love Regained: a Periodic Sentence
At a fairyfly-like moment
On a bushy corner of nature
Preferably under a tall pine tree
In Mayuehe, our mecca or the hilly village
Adjacent closely to the bank of the Yangtze River
With myriad tongues from my hungry innermost being
Each eager to reach deep into your heart, where my soul's
Fingers could caress every single synapse of your feminine
feel
Between the warmth & tenderness of love, across the
Pacific & the Pandemic
I'll join you

HOW COULD YOU
Marissa Garofalo

How could you forget
all of the promises
you made?

Promises of the present and future
promises of hope.

How could you say
you actually loved me?

Loved me so much
yet you turned your back on me
as I watched you walk away.

How could you not care?

Care about the life you created?
Care what happens in my life?

How could you walk away as a
parent?

I have a purpose
I have a plan
My life has a future with or
without you.

WORTHLESS
Marissa Garofalo

Dark night skies
Fading into daylight.

Ever so cold
as the shadows return
to the darkness.
The thought of uncertainty
leaves my mind.
Feelings of worthlessness
leave my soul as I take
my first breath of the new day.
The sun shines
through all of my pain
it brings hope to
my soul.
Every beam of the sun
breaks through all of my pain.
it gives me hope for the next step
of my new life.

DARKEST HOUR
Marissa Garofalo

It's dark,
pure dark.
I sit on this dock
all alone.
You know the darkest of night
right before dusk.
The darkest hour of being
in a deep depressed thought.
All you want to do is
cry.
But you also wonder why?
I hate the darkest hour
it happens often.
As the tears flow
the pain is released.
I remember the happiest of times
of the life I leave behind.

FADING
Marissa Garofalo

Fading into the abyss of darkness
Afraid of what I will miss.
Entering into the world alone
Who knows what will hold?
Slipping into a deep sleep
Who knows who will keep my soul safe?
Fading into the known
Fearing the absolute unknown of my life.

DEAD PLANET
Marissa Garofalo

Earth is still
the night is calm.
What is coming
to kill?
Killing the purest form of
happiness that
lingers in us all.
The happiness that we
once knew as children.
Why must it die?
Once we see the true earth.
How sad it is?
We try to change it with hope but,
the darkness takes over.

JUST A GIRL
Marissa Garofalo

Lost In a deep thought
She smiles to let the
World know she's ok.

A beautiful smile
Hides
How beautifully broken
Her soul Is.

How tormented she is
On the inside.

She wears a smile just
To feel a glimmer of hope
In a world she desperately
Wants to be a part of.

A **world** that does not want her.

HER
Marissa Garofalo

Alone in a tiny coffee shop
in a city
on a corner

Lost in a thought
about the memories of
the life she once lived.

She is exquisite
blonde hair
golden as the sun

Skin ever so white
as if it were a fresh
bed of snow.

Her dress as green as the
grass in the springtime
When she walks, it is like
a smooth wave crashing.

She speaks as if
she were singing a song.
When she becomes angry
her wrath will be felt
Like the lightening hitting the ground.
Like the clouds clashing in the heavens.

ANNABEL LEE BREAKS HER SILENCE BY THE SEA

— Inspired by "Annabel Lee," the last complete poem written by Edgar Allan Poe

LindaAnn LoSchiavo

It was too many years ago that he,
Dishonorably discharged, introduced
Himself to me. I ran a B and B
Then: "Kingdom by the Sea" in Miami.

He claimed he'd shield me from the "Tyranny
Of Ordinary." I replied, "Can you
Clean drains, fix pipes with a mortician's care?"
"Winged seraphs," he sighed, adding, "Sounds dreamy."

He wasn't in touch with reality,
Describing my inn as a sepulcher.
Since this is Florida, the morbid term
Eluded tourists. Still. It rankled me.

His nihilism had reached the nth degree,
Always contemplating mortality.
A swell mechanic, sure, but his morose
Mindset was only fit for poetry.

Then hurricanes uprooted my palm trees,
Chilling and killing income by the sea,
Chilling and killing my prized B and B.
While sweeping up debris, we disagreed.

Storm winds rushed me into the sounding sea.
How strange. He calls me bride, sees my bright eyes,
Mourns by my sepulcher built near the sea.

Famous, he's published now by FSG.

A KISS IN THE DARK
John A. Taylor

If you want to be scared, come with me
Don't look in the closet
Don't look under the stair
If you come with me, you'll find your scare
Ignore that creaking door and the shadows moving across the drawn shade
And the goose flesh on your arm there
Come along with me, I'll even hold your hand, and together we'll find a scare
The shapes and faces you're seeing in the dark, and the child's tattered dolly sitting in the chair
It's all a mirage, follow me, and I'll show you the scare
The stranger standing outside your window, the one with the maniac's stare
He's not even close to horror, nor close to the real scare
We're close now
Yes, here we are
Take firm grip of my hand
Breathe in the air
Kiss me, it's the only way
You wanted it, and here it is
For you and I to share

SUSTENANCE
John A. Taylor

It is your eyes that I crave
Dark pools mottled with patina
And now exquisite crimson
And your throat!
Slender, muscular, your pulse is strong here
But weakening
And lastly, your thigh
There...high where only I may linger
Hidden by lace from all but me
Your trusted lover
I'll only take a few select pieces
An expert butcher am I
My murderer's blade is always sharpest
For those whom I adore
Happy Valentine's Day, m'dear

THE LADY ACROSS THE MEADOW
John A. Taylor

I see her there
Every midnight
Across this dead and dying meadow
My yard, my resting place
Apparition or bone and tissue?
Classic cheeks either reflect or contain a fine ruddy hue
Her lips are dark and stoic
A perfect line broken only in one place
Where her top lip turns up in one corner
Is it a smile?
Or is it a roach trying to escape her mouth?
From this distance, I cannot determine
Is she a mirage or a
Message attempting contact from beyond the meadow?
A last, desperate call from those still there?
If she would only speak!
Break the still plane of her crooked mouth and tell me…
Something!
Where do I go from here?
Do I go from here?
Screams of protest draw no response
I surrender
And wait
A thought: perhaps this is my hell!
A never ending unanswered question
Oh, how cruel
Oh, how deserved
No joyous ending
No certainty determined
Only the two of us

Silent, staring at one another
Across my dying meadow
My resting place
I have eternity to solve the mystery
I wonder, does she?

HOME AT LAST
Bill Evans

Clickety-clack
The hoven hoofs
Echoed
Through the dungeon corridor
Announcing
He who would be a god
Or demi-god
Champion of sinners
Not saved
A black god
With a black genius
And a black goddess
With black sapphires
Drinking in the hatred
As his face turned
The color of despair

NOT GOING HOME
Bill Evans

Crows…no…scarecrows
Wading in the gray water

Orbs of light
Everywhere
Angry lost souls

##
Bill Evans

Redundant guerilla warfare

Blinded by delusion

My least favorite wheat field
Graves of plastic soldiers

Where is the decency?

POWER
Bill Evans

The pied piper walked backwards
As the world looked on in horror
And shrieked
-only too late
Much too late

All of the goodwill credits earned were not redeemable
An ill-conceived rouse
As those with faith had become faithless
Promises broken
Truths being furiously unlearned

Would the piper stop? Please?
Was it possible?
Please just stop!

I had become
Judge
Jury
And (self)
Executioner

LILITH
Bill Evans

Shining beacon to the awakened
The first serpent
Unbending to patriarchal superiority
Perceiver of
Wolves disguised as lambs
Tricks disguised as miracles
Goddess-mother of fertility
Including the fallen angels
And the impure
 denied admission
To all realms
Of heaven
or hell

She is not mine
 belonging to no one
Shaped from clay
Unyielding
Unapologetic
Gloriously defiant
Temptress
Avenger
Mother of demons
Shunned by the Nazarene
…and scorned by men
Stop searching for access warrior mother
The large entrance
With no barriers for entry
Has denied you a ticket
For admission
To the rapturous glee of enlightenment

Or the bathing flames of the forsaken

King Minos is a cruel judge
His pronged tail lashing
With violent spasms
Thrusting the traitors
With their frozen tears
Into Hell's 9th circle
A toothless conqueror
Exposing all of the evils
While denying you most glorious queen
A glorious death

INNER DEMONS
Chris McAuley

I stand at the platform.
Waiting impatiently for the train.
I am screaming inside.
My tortured mind is issuing long piercing howls.
I can't control my hands as they ball into fists.
I raise them to my head.
The nightmares still continue however.

Beaten by my mother for failing the test at school.
Hounded by my boss for the final report.
Watching my wife's smile as she leaves me.
My face burning as she touches the hand of my brother.

The platform begins to fill with people.
None of them can hear the screams which have been
shaking my senses for the last three years.
Since I have left Collage, there has been no respite from
them.
The voices manifest and echo in my mind.

Smiling gentle at those around me.
I appear affable and polite.
My suit is pressed and my umbrella furled.
I have always been able to blend in.
My fellow travelers have no idea that within their midst.
Lurks a vicious killer.

This was to be my first murder.
I had resisted it for so long.
Attempting to drown the voices out with cheap whiskey and
beer.

Tablets prescribed by doctors.
Expensive sex sold at street corners.

The train approaches and my mind reels.
I see umbrellas unfurling, mouths cursing the ever-changing British climate.
I see a balding man in a green raincoat ahead of me.
He sneezes into a tissue.
The voices in my mind halt their cacophony as I made a decision.

I move closer to the man as the train grows closer.
The tracks vibrate and a collective anticipation grows.
For some this signifies the reassurance of the journey home.
For one this will be their final destination.

The train makes its entrance.
Its grey frame seems like a bullet as it emerges from the tunnel.
Turning around the bend at terrific speed.
A feeling like needles pricking the backs of my eye sockets.
The voices begin to return.
The screaming in my mind begins again.
Images of past failings overwhelm me.

The train is hurtling into the station.
There is a sigh of disappointment from the platform.
This is not their train.
I smiled.
It was mine.

I suppress the urge to vomit as I move towards the man in front of me.
Fear and desire mix and I feel the thrashing of my stomach.
Closer I move to the green anorak.

I catch sight of the man's shocked face as I run past him.
Thinking of his possible wife and family as I pick up pace.
Homely comforts and a midweek glass of wine by the fireside.

Moving faster than I had ever thought possible.
I am running for freedom.
Jumping onto the tracks, I hear the shocked expressions of those I leave behind.
At this, my end, I pray for darkness and peace.

ON A KNIFE EDGE
Chris McAuley

Criminal Poetry
I watched the train depart from the station.
The sound of its staccato movement gave a halting voice to thoughts.
Darkness had been swelling in my mind from the events of this morning.
I turned to face the heavy rain and from my coat pulled a knife.
I had taken it from the deli counter from the supermarket where I worked.
This isn't a story about the rich and famous or about love-stained sheets.
This is a tale of the madness which comes from betrayal.

I have to hurry; I might miss my chance.
I want to see her face.
To smell her delicate perfume.
To embrace her closely once more.

I was once a husband.
I had a wonderful wife who thought of every detail.
She was thoughtful and kind.
She planned our every moment, from future trips to our dream home.
This all came to an end when the delivery arrived this morning.
A small brown box which was tied with a red bow.
A package which was both inauspicious and gaudy.

I round the corner.
My heart lurching in tandem with my stomach.

Butterflies skitter inside as I feel faint with excitement.
I feared that I might already be too late.
As I glimpse the restaurant at the end of the street.
The smell of seafood fills the air.
I tear my foggy glasses from my face.
I want to look at her with a naked and unfocused gaze.
To see her as I did at our first moment of meeting.

Inside the box was a series of Polaroids
The Polaroids contained pictures of my wife in various stages of undress.
As she disrobed, a smile emerged.
Her secret smile which I thought she had only reserved for me.
When I saw the sixth picture, my heart shattered entirely.
A man emerged, in a matching state of nakedness.
He smiled too, but not with his lips.

There she is.
She is glancing at her watch.
I slick my wet hair from my face and begin to run.
She sees me approach.
Her face shows none of the customary welcome I am used to as I return home.
Instead, it registers shock.
I can see her mouth begin to move, lips attempting to sync an excuse in tandem with her thoughts.
I slow down and smile.

I reach out and touch her cheek. Her amber hair tumbles from the hood of her rain jacket.
I bought her that last winter at a department store in the city.
She loved the floral pattern emblazed on its front.
It's funny how seemingly meaningless things present themselves in the forefront of your mind at moments like this.

I lean forward and hear a vague story about meeting a colleague from her university book club.

As I hold her body close to mine, I raise the knife.
Thrusting it downward, I hold her tightly.
I support her flailing legs and begin the motion again.
Her blood spurts into the rain and onto the street.
Quickly washing away into the drain.
Soon the body becomes heavy, I let her slowly drop to the ground.
As she does so, I give her one last lingering kiss.
Laying her frame to the ground, I vaguely hear the screams of passers-by
As I turn and walk forward and into the unending rain.

THE VOID OF CREATION
Chris McAuley

The artist in search of grace.
Finds the pit of darkness the special place.
As they peer into the void.
They discover the inspiration from the bleakness that others avoid.

The empty page is a call to the soul.
To convey the emotions which we can no longer control.
The demons inside rage.
To these hellish spirits I must pay my wage.

I have never loved one such as you before.
When you left me, it shook my soul to its core.
I watch you holding another's face.
Asking myself was I so very easy to replace?

I stand upon the gallows in my room.
The noose pulled tight to seal my doom.
As I rock off the chair.
I ask myself if you ever cared.

The rope bites and cuts.
My phone buzzes and interrupts.
I glance over and kick uselessly in the air.
Your picture has appeared, I offer it as my last prayer.

THE TURNING KEY IN MY MIND
Chris McAuley

I have turned the key and locked away.
All the thoughts and memories of that tragic day.
Now I stand outside that obsidian rooms door.
I finally turn my back upon the one I adore.

I pile against that room so many things.
Pleasures and pain, the treasures of forgotten kings.
Yet still I return here once more.
I can never ignore her, the one that I adore.

ANGER
Chris McAuley

I stand stunned unable to believe what you just said.
You tell me that you are miserable.
I just don't know how that could be.
I gave you everything I had.
How the hell could you claim to be so sad?

I watched you cry as you told your tale.
Your sky-blue eyes dripping rain across your bronzed face.
I listen and try to hear.
The truth is that I have had too much beer.

I had raged and raved.
Really, I had no right to demand.
I was young and thought you, my prize.
The truth is that you deserved your freedom.

Older now and we pass on the street.
I take a chance and move towards you to speak.
I apologize for those past times.
We converse and reminisce about the changes in our lives.

Anger is a beast which seeks to control.
Dark envy a paragon of lust and nothing more.
Regret can be a pathway to wisdom.
Love is the understanding of perfect freedom.

THE SWINGER'S LAMENT
T. L. Barrett

I met her in a tavern, far from home.
She seemed a creature from some mythic tome.

Scaled, she slithered toward me, eyes a-fire,
but the patrons only gaped in desire.

"What are you?" I stuttered, trembled and shook.
Her smile showed fangs as she gave me a look.

"No worries, cutie. You've nothing to fear.
I won't be feeding on you; you're a seer."

How many men take such a prideful fall?
"You're special," she purred. I was in her thrall.

She dragged me to her nest, there we mated.
Not long after, we cohabitated.

The wedding was a terror, sheer agony to the end,
keeping her from brother, cousin and friend.

She surprised me that night, and bound me tight
and told me to watch an unholy sight.

She called for room service. Some young strapping guy
fell to her charms, like a man fixed to die.

She moaned, he moaned, I moaned just to see it,
while she fed on his blood, essence and spit.

He begged for release, while she ate his junk.

After, he slumped in a most vapid funk.

She slapped him, he stirred, he walked from the room,
a zombie, forever trudging toward doom.

I've learnt to appreciate it a bit,
watching the cocky turn into a twit.

But it's hell keeping satisfied a fiend,
who'd happily turn to neighbor and friend.

So weekends it's clubs or some rich guy's house.
They'll give up their souls to take off her blouse.

I've seen the lamia who is my wife
deprive three strong men of spirit and life.

And though they may rise up from the stained ground,
their fire's out, not one soul to be found.

I've begged: "Take me!" She freezes in place,
then slithers and licks the salt from my face.

She loves me, I suppose, in her strange way,
but I know why with me she holds at bay.

She sees herself reflected in my eyes,
so if she drinks from such a soul, she dies.

I'm not certain whether I hate her or love her,
but of this I am certain: we deserve each other.

She'll take her meal from those she'll fuck and flirt.
While I, with tears and pain, provide dessert.

THE WOMAN IN QUESTION
Ed Ahern

I am close to a woman
bruised in an unknowable way,
who presents herself to me
as cordial and supportive,
but to others even closer
as hate-filled and vindictive,
and does not seem to see
the contradictions of her nature.

It's not her conscious fault
to indulge in abscessed discord
but it is her delusion to feel wronged
by those subject to her presence,
and her fate to bruise those
drawn to her attractiveness.

STORY OF MOIRA
Veronica Kegel-Giglio

Let's just say that she loved me too much
Moira called me every day, harped, followed
She tried arranging everything for me and changing me
She cooed and fondled me too much
It was gross and got on my nerves
She would not let me go
I tried everything to get rid of her
But she got no hints
Finally, I told her the truth
I told her I was in love with someone else
Moira was furious
She flew into a rage screaming and attacking me
Wailing that nobody else could love me like she did
When she lunged at me with a knife, I shot and killed her
Now she haunts my bedroom at night
No matter who I am with or what I am doing, she comes
Haunting me always
No, she can never let me go
That is a fact that I know

WE MADE A FOREVER PACT
Veronica Kegel-Giglio

I was in a sanatorium because they said I was crazy
I drank morning, noon, and night to forget all the abuse
He was a drug addict committed for attacking a relative
He said the relative had raped him, but nobody believed or cared
We understood each other in that crazy asylum
It was a scary place where residents were part of experiments and died strange deaths
Some of them disappeared, and others ran away
Screams and fights filled the air at night, but we clung to each other
We loved each other and were soul mates
We promised each other we would always love one another and stay together
Sometimes we fought because we loved each other so
Petty jealousies and insecurities sometimes broke into our relationship
One day he accused me of flirting with a guard and being a whore
I stabbed and killed him in a fit of rage
Then I killed myself
I could not walk the earth without him
However, now we both haunt the crazy sanatorium nut house together
We haunt there, and we haunt the crazy relatives who wronged us
We are happy now as ghosts
Always together

HER GREATEST LOVE
Veronica Kegel-Giglio

She would tell you that he was the greatest love of her life
He listened to her sing and watched her dance with enthusiasm
He told her she was beautiful and that there was no other on earth like her
She loved his gifts and his praise
He took her to wonderful restaurants and theatrical shows
There was not a time when their lovemaking was not erotic and fine
However, when he told her that he could never leave his wife for her
She went berserk and could not stop herself
She had to have him with her forever
So she killed him brutally with a knife, but kept his body in her bed
Then he could never leave her
He could never return to his wife and family
She was now his family
She kept him in that bed as he decomposed into a skeleton
Constantly, she sang love songs and recited poetry to his dead corpse
But she was happy in that bloody bed with him in it
Years passed, but she did not realize it
She had him there all to herself
When they found her in the bed clutching his bones
She was old and dead, but she had a smile on her face

HE TOLD ME TO DO IT
Veronica Kegel-Giglio

I fell head over heels in love with her
She was so beautiful and she captured my heart
She laughed at my ventriloquist act and cooked and cleaned for me
She loved my Danny doll and complimented my talents constantly
Sex with her was so fantastic that I begged her to move into the apartment
Then she began whining about an engagement ring, marriage, and her needs
Her needs required more and more money
She began to steal my things and my credit cards
Her nagging demands became too much, and Danny told me to get rid of her
So I killed her just like he told me to do, and I buried her body in the woods
But now Danny tells me to kill every woman I get serious about
And I cannot stop the killing now

I AM THE DOLL THAT WATCHES OUT FOR HER
Veronica Kegel-Giglio

I loved him so much and did all that he asked
Others tried to warn me how dangerous he was, but I did not care
He beat and belittled me, and I continued to love him too much
He got me pregnant, and I gave birth to our daughter
Then he raged his disappointment and killed me
My spirit now lives in the body of our daughter's favorite doll
I want to be near her and try to protect her as best I can.
I do not want her to suffer my fate
I do not want love to go wrong for her or for her to die an untimely death
I will find a way to always protect her

LOVELY LADY IN THE WINDOW
Veronica Kegel-Giglio

In a small town, there once lived a man with an evil wife
She made his life miserable and would never let him go
Later, the man fell in love with a woman of lovely physique and character from another town
This lovely lady loved him as much as he did her
She waited for him night after night by the window of her second floor bedroom
He always came to her
However, their love was doomed and killed them both
Her body was found mutilated and decapitated, and his was found not long after
The evil wife disappeared
Either she killed them, or they had a suicide pact
Nobody knows
However, the lady's ghost can be seen at night in the second floor bedroom window
And her lover's ghost is standing behind her

LOVER DOLL
Veronica Kegel-Giglio

She loved him so much. She only wanted to be his one and only

She sang to him, cooked for him, and cleaned for him

And she would always tell him how much she loved him

When he told her one night after dinner that he had fallen in love with another

She said nothing, but she poisoned him instead and hid his ashes inside her doll

She carried that doll with her always and sang songs to it

She told others he had gone on a long business trip

Then she told others he had gotten very sick

After awhile they stopped asking about him

And she sang love songs to her beloved doll with the ashes

And she told all how much she loved him

She is still carrying him around with her everywhere she goes

FOR THE QUEST OF LOVE
Veronica Kegel-Giglio

I only wanted you to love me and see my inner beauty and magnificent soul

I wanted you to want intimacy with me

However, you rejected me and my loving gestures, praises, and gifts

You mocked my ugly face and disfigured body, and I could not bear it

So I killed you and hid your body where nobody could find it

Unfortunately, when I pursued my next love, the same things happened

So again, I killed her and buried the body

Now, I really am a monster

I am now ugly inside and outside

And all because no woman loved or accepted me

My quest for love made me a real monster

So now, my quest for love makes me hunt and kill at night

BESPELL MY HEART
Brianna Malotke

Stolen glances, and sweet
murmured affections were
how he melted her heart.

His smile and soft touches,
whether holding hands or
gently rubbing her back, were
how he bespelled her heart.

Whispered promises and
passionate kisses were
how he finally won her heart.

But here alone, with her
packed bags, waiting in the
dark outside her home, the
agreed upon time had passed

several hours ago, and in
this very moment, was
how he broke her heart.

DECAYING HEARTACHE
Brianna Malotke

The moonlight peeked through
The gap in her heavy velvet curtains,
Her room was pitch black, with
Just a sliver of light illuminating
Her carpet, like a dagger shining,
She tried to sleep, but her mind
Was restless and her body was
Aching for his touch, though
As she lay in bed alone, with
The silence enveloping her,
She at least found some solace
That although her heart was
Broken, he had shattered it into
Pieces, it would heal over time,
While his would slowly be decaying
Somewhere deep within the woods,
Buried with her darkest secrets.

LATEST HOME RENOVATION
Brianna Malotke

She sipped her hot coffee,
Enjoying the quiet weekend
Morning by herself, knowing
With time her heart would heal.

They had chosen the house
Together, with all of its faults
And all of its quirks, it was theirs.

On one crisp autumn evening
She had found him in bed with
Another, while they had worked
Together to fix up the home,
They just couldn't fix this.

Her heart heavy, only one
Solution came to mind, and so
She carried out her plan, the
Latest renovation to their home.

While every day forward she
Would be lonely, at least she
Would never truly be alone.

For he was buried beneath
The new wine cellar, forever
A piece of the home – and
her heart – so you see she'd
Never really be alone.

GHOST
C.M. Godbout

You left as quickly as you came—
without warning, a thief in the night.
You were surreptitious, furtive,
riddled with a mixture of guilt and longing.

And now, like a ghost of my past,
you come back to haunt me
when the nights are dark and long
and I lay in bed, alone.

Once, we promised each other forever
like naïve, innocent children,
oblivious to the world around us,
unaware of the threatening storm ahead.

In the midst of the tempest, I picked up the pieces
and sold my soul to hold us together.
But storms have their way of destroying everything,
everything that is precious to me.

Now, I am left with nothing but memories—
pictures, songs, the bracelet you gave me
that still rests on my nightstand, a memento
of a love I thought would never die.

I only have these tainted memories,
so bittersweet that I can taste them
when they drip down my cheeks, onto my lips,
the same lips that once kissed your own.

You have left a permanent mark on my troubled heart,

and no amount of whiskey can wash away my lovesickness.
My mind wanders to you, and I don't know how to deal with
the fact that you don't love me anymore.

I must sleep now; I haven't slept
in days, weeks, months, forever.
I can handle nightmares, but seeing you in my dreams
is the worst kind of hell imaginable.

Please don't meet me in dreamland
when I drift off to sleep tonight.
I can't take another night of torture from you,
my ghost, who is never in sight but always there.

AFTER YOU DIED
Karen Demmans

I never thought I would miss
Seven digits in a row
The one thing consistent
Through many years of change
Now I will never again
Pick up a phone to dial
That one same phone number

RIPPED
Karen Demmans

I carry the burden
Of your soul
Knowing there is nothing
That could've saved you
Ripped from me
In your time of need
Your heart taken
But never forgotten

TATTOO
Karen Demmans

Your tattoo
Upon your shoulder
The beautiful mark
That makes it you
A sign I can see
From a mile away
As your flesh decays
And you stumble around
Your brain gone primal
Your hunger consumes you
But your tattoo
Still makes it you
I never miss when I shoot
But I will miss you

WYD?
Karen Demmans

You must be single
You keep lighting up my phone
I'm not your backup

COME WITH ME
Sarah Kay Collie

Come in.
I made a whole world.
It's everything this one isn't.
Some say it's pretend.
I will admit it is comprised of fiction.
But.
It's where you live.
It's not broken.
In this world I don't have to walk barefoot through trauma.
Instead we dance barefoot in the backyard.
Holding on.
In this world.
We never have to let go.
So come.
Stay a while.
We aren't allowed very long.
The only way in is through sweet sleep.
But.
Come with me.
I made a whole world.
It's where you live, my love.
I made a whole world.
It's everything this one isn't.

WASH ME
Sarah Kay Collie

Wash me
Clean me
Take this blood and pain from me
Drown me beneath my tears
That I can be born new
So I can be loved again
I'm filthy from this pain

MY SOUL
Sarah Kay Collie

So familiar.
Like a home.
One I have always lived in.
Walking around in the dark.
No need for a light.
My soul.
So familiar.
Until our love.
Everything shifted.
Just enough.
To need a few candles lit.
 My soul.
So familiar.
Still home.
But it was ours.
But to lose this love.
To lose you.
My soul.
No longer a home.
Forever changed.
Every light on.
I recognize nothing.
I can't find my way.
My soul.
It is no home.
Just a place.
It's mine still.
Mine to mourn in.
Haunted now.
My soul every light on.
Praying for the dark.

Praying for it to be a home like it once was.
My soul.
It is no home.

IT WAVES AT YOU
Victor Marrow

He waved at me from behind the stop sign,
Hues of hatred leaked from his smile,
My terror trickled across nerve endings frayed by hope,
No one listened as I shouted at his shadow.
He stared at me as my dad took his last breath,
Long gray fingertips tapped on tombstones of everyone I knew,
His dark circumference suffocated all hope, all light,
An unforgiven stain of existence.
He whispered to me during my clash with cancer,
Each hospital visit he peeked from the window,
Protruding nostrils flared at my emaciated physique,
Licked his lips each doomed test result.
Tonight, doorknobs and windows rattle, he comes for me,
Subterranean toenails clatter across my unkept wooden floors,
Above my headboard his guttural hisses soak my final moments,
My fight to cling to the earth's flesh is lost, darkened laughter into eternity.

BLUE + GREEN = RED
Hansen Tor Adcock

A searching gaze,
blue as the infant's eyes straight after the birth canal,
as surgical gloves,
nitrogen, as planets too far from the Sun,
my brother's favourite marbles, unpolluted waters,
blue as neon tetra fish, as Frank Sinatra's handkerchief,
bruises from that tumble downstairs,
blue as my walls,
as hypoxia, as the sky's zenith in the middle of August,
blue as depression
and the ghost of your smile.

You search for yourself in a place that is not her.

She turns green in her heart,
green as aliens, as undisturbed grasses,
as Old Man's Beard and vines hanging from trees in Louisiana swamps,
as mould on two-week-old bread, as money,
the marbles my brother lost down the back of the sofa, as seaweed,
as milk's edges, as rotting wood,
venus fly-traps and the backs of starlings,
greener than innocence and spring,
than hedgerows in Eden,

And soon, the world turns red,

Redder than rage and love,
fire, blood, lava,
molten iron, the Earth's core,

capsaicin and volcano casserole,

Leaving everything blackened charcoal except my heart,

Which is blue,
helpless blue.

INTROSPECTION
Alexander Etheridge

Hell-storm overtaking the hills,
the blistering rain comes forever now.

Listen in the new black dawn
to the end of space and time.

Hellfire all around, a hurricane of dust and fire.
The seas dried up just before the sun was lost.

Look into the doom of red stars, darkening
stars, and thrashing hail. Look into

the horror in the mirror becoming
the horror in the world.

WINTER NIGHTMARE
Alexander Etheridge

The sky here is gun-metal gray, sunken
and frigid to the touch. You can hear the heat

evaporating, you can feel the sound of
rising winds, you can taste

the feel of gusting sleet---It's been centuries in the ice
and freezing rains. God knows

nothing of this place, and everything here
is blind with blue wind-frost. So little

survives the blizzarding dawns.
Our forests are are bent over and torn

in the rime, the last ocean froze over.
Our stars burn a cold red, our dreams burn

the last of our books for warmth. Hailstones
fly through ruined churches.

This world, cold since birth and long abandoned,
has abandoned itself to its only season.

PATCHWORK
Shawna Renée Lewis

I walked so long
In a daze.
Not knowing you were poison.
Then I broke
Never thought
a body could hold
a broken soul.
Ignored,
by those who could not watch
Others,
watching me.
Waiting!
To see if my body would fall too.
Instead,
I used
An invisible needle
to stitch myself up
with parts
put back upside down
Inside out.
From random pieces
That aren't mine.
I am no longer the girl you made with fear.
I am the woman
I patched together
the one who I like now.

DARK BALLAD OF LOST LOVE
Max Bindi

She was a beautiful blight
strange all right
deadly and wild
half immortal and half alive
you know those kind of things
that never die
cause they are hardly born
believe me I poured all my blood
on the altar of her body and soul
and being loved back to death
was the seal of my final downfall

Don't cheer me up
now the time is dead and gone
her black love is in my cup
my flesh is stripped to the bone
Don't cheer me up
now the time is dead and gone
my skull is on her lap
She carved my name on her heart of stone
The phantom we never saw
sang unearthly spooky songs
said I'm gonna tell you
what you have always known

Love will live forever
all lovers must die alone
Oh, don't cheer me up
now the time is dead and gone
her black love is in my cup
my flesh is stripped to the bone

Oh, don't cheer me up
now the time is dead and gone
this lost love story
is half of her demons
and half of my own.

THE DOWNFALL
Gerardo Serrano R

Once I had a dream,
Which took control of my life,
And made my worst nightmares come true.

The Nocturnal Bird, idealistic, ignored,
The truthful sign of light:
The truer springhead from all life.

Its knowledge was restricted
Only to darkness and death;
However, one day that changed,
Annihilating his life forevermore.

One day that was surprised by a celestial fire,
Slumbering and hidden in its warren,
Its face nabbed with its luminary.
At first, it blinded it
And it was left on the verge of losing its reason;
It felt fear of seeing itself,
Exposed and defenseless,
Before the sight of everyone.

Little by little, that changed;
That found out a wonderful world,
That couldn't believe its existence.
--The bird loved the light, loved loving it.

At that very moment, it thought:
--My dream came to its ending.
Finally, it was the moment,
With great courage, it plucked enough bravery,

And through the real got into;
But how mistaken it was.

The bird loved the beautiful light,
Loved loving it so much.
So, it decided to undertake flight in its direction,
So it could be closer to it.

And as long as it rose high;
It felt his comforting heat.
It never knew such a warmth;
Its whole experience was
Only nocturnal chilliness.
It felt to belong to that world,
To that cosmos of light and life.

It flew high upwards to its direction, your direction,
Swollen with hope and pride,
Intoxicated with bliss;
It felt how the pleasure grew up in it,
And each time that it was approaching it,
To that very light, it could feel
Something never lived before.
It lavished it with glow, security,
Which was able to sense.
It felt to belong to something greater,
To the world, to color, and life.
Yes, your blessed life.

And the bird was exposed to the sight of all,
After being remained hidden.
Its atramentous plumage shone,
Reflexing such precious glittering from your eyes.
And the bird flew higher and higher:
And it was more shining, more blinding.

Just to be able to reach you.

It flew towards that bright,
The dream seemed to be coming true at last
At last, it turned into a nightmare.
For there, exposed, at the sight of everybody.
Everyone could watch this ominous being,
Flying towards the light,
This bugbear, this ugly freak
This damned monster doomed
to dwell forever in hell.

The bird felt for the first time in its life,
As if it were real; but when it touched the light,
Yes, your blessed light,
It found out the truth hidden from it:
--It didn't find what it had hoped for.

The shimmering hurt it,
As nothing had hurt it before.
It was a subtle snare: --Your light hurt it and burned it,
The bird fell ablaze emitting shrieks.
Its flesh was burning alive, it burned alive.

Thus it began its fall, the falling of the nocturnal bird.
It ignored it –its place was next to hell,
Not heaven above next to you.

When it fell, filled with pain; it knew the truth of all;
It didn't belong to this bright world,
Its place lay next to the mire; not on the surface.

It didn't belong to the cosmos of life,
But to a dark and rotten hell
--It paid for its effrontery and vanity—so dearly.

It fell to the deepest well,
A place where reigned the night eternally.
There it fell the bird on the soil,
Mauled and wounded,
Deformed by sores and damages,
Blisters and scars that covered it all over,
Its ugly and nasty being,
Yes, poor little freak.

It turned into a maze of scars,
And everyone mocked at its silly vanity.
It was transformed into the direst of beings
That dwelled in the night:
--Everybody laughed at its scurrilousness.

Now, filled with rage and hatred,
It dashed against everything that meant light and life;
Against whoever had rejected it and wounded it.

My dream came to an end, the bird returned to its world,
To never, go out again, nevermore.

I am the bird enslaved by night,
Filled with a grudge against the living;
That has excluded me from your tastiest deserts,
Causing repulsion to all creatures, beautiful and pretty:
--Gods of the subtle and from the sweet world of light,
Which would be frightened by my horrendous shape.

I never believe this would finish like this;
In your light, I felt freer than ever before;
In your light, I felt more alive than ever before;
That the universe had a sense and reason:
--Why things are never as I want them to be!

EVERYTHING FOR NOTHING
Serena Daniels

I thought I was in love
So I left it all behind
Saw nothing of my old world
And walked blindly into yours
Into darkness I came
Believing I could bring you to light
For you to do the same as me
I was patient
I was giving
I was loving
But I was a fool
I gave, gave and gave
And you took, took, took
With no intention to reciprocate
To never give back
I will give you one last thing
I will release you from this life
Either as reward or punishment
For me giving you everything
And it was all for nothing

ALL CHOKED UP
Josh Darling

I came to the
Park Nai Lert Hotel,
because I heard
it was haunted.

That's right,
weeks ago,
I reserved suite 352,
and bought a $1,600
plane ticket,
to fly
from:
Providence, Rhode Island
to:
Bangkok, Thailand.

I say Providence,
because it's not just a place,
it's a word with meaning,
giving it more weight than,
LaGuardia International Airport.

Bangkok is hot,
and wet.
This weather
is only suitable for the perverts
who come here for
the underage ladyboys.

I was here
for a ghost.

--And the air conditioning.

Holy fuck,
it's hot.

I've spent my entire life
wanting to see a ghost.
I know it wouldn't prove anything.
But damn
it would make a great a story.
As would flying around the world
20 hours on a plane,
to see one.

The internet was full
of postings about this hotel.
But the ghost hunting TV shows,
wanted nothing to do with it.

Getting to suite 352,
I turned out the lights,
I drew the curtains,
and waited.

--In the dark, that's the only way to do it.

They talk about haunting,
having a connection to:
murder
unrequited romance
unfinished earthly business.

It wasn't until midnight
that I heard it:
A gentle,

fap, fap, fap…
coming from the closet.
The door was locked,
I knew,
I was alone.
It didn't stop,
the,
fap, fap, fap…
continued.

I got out of bed,
unsure of what to do.
I knew if I turned on the light,
I wouldn't be able to see it.
This is how everyone
described
the beginning of their encounter,
fap, fap, fap…
Rising to my feet,
I stepped
toward the closet.
Extending my hand,
I reached for the closet's
door knob.

fap, fap, fap…

I turned the handle,

fap, fap, fap…

Opening the door,
I saw him.
David Carradine.
The actor from Kung-Fu

and
Kill Bill,
masturbating with one hand
choking himself with a length of rope
with the other.

fap, fap, fap…
"Help me finish!"
the ghost shouted.

But I couldn't.
Scared,
and a coward,
I ran,
hoping to never hear
the dreaded sound of
fapping
again.

JACK THE RIPPER
Josh Darling

He has knife for a cock and he loves making it with the ladies.
He is drunk and covered with blood and cum and naked except for his top hat.
He cuts his fingers to the bone every time he jerks offs.
Don't you want a date lady?

He's sick of pornography wants a return to fundamental values.
He wants to see what you're made of on the inside even before you date.
He's gonna see your guts and he'll use his dick to cut right to them.
Don't you want a date lady?

I love you so much I want no one else to have you,
let's keep you whole and pure,
let's keep your reputation upright,
let's see your guts,
let's see your blood,
I got a knife for a cock and I'll fuck right done dead.
Don't you want a date lady?

YOU'RE GOING TO DIE TAKING A SHIT
Josh Darling

I don't want to mislead you with the title of this poem.
It's about how you're going to die
–hypothetically.

I had a friend,
He worked as an EMT,
Sometimes,
he'd get called,
when someone found a dead relative.
He told me,
most of the time of the time,
they'd find elderly people,
always naked,
half the time they'd crapped the bed.
The other half of the time,
they were on the toilet.
They died,
of heart attacks from trying to force a shit out of their asses.

This poem is not about that kind
of death shit.
Though that is one
–hypothetical.

The shit I'm talking about,
the one that will kill you,
is the survivalist shit.
Every now and then,
some young man,
usually white,
usually with a cubical job,

always from the city or the suburbs,
starts up a conversation with me
that starts out something like,

"Wouldn't the zombie apocalypse be great?"

And my answer is always the same,
"If it did, you'd die taking a shit."

And they don't get it.

Taking a shit during the zombie apocalypse
will be the death of more people,
than the starvation,
than the gangs of marauders,
or the killer zombies themselves.
The first thing that's going to go,
is the toilet paper.
When society is truly done,
there will be nothing to wipe your ass with.
That's what the anarchist want,
their meetings aren't about blowing up banks,
or the end of the forced social contract.
What they really discus at anarchists meets is an end of ass wiping.
And an end of ass wiping
is what the zombie apocalypse is really about.

When that last square of Charmin,
that Charmin you used to squeeze,
is gone…

That's when you die.

You'll tell your group of friends,

"Hey, I gotta go into the wood
and take a break for moment,"
or maybe you'll just be crass and say,
"I gotta take a shit."

And into the woods you'll head.
A way from your party…
And you'll be dropping a duce,
In the middle of the woods,
with birds and squirrels watching you,
face all red.
Grunting one out of your turd cutter.
Simultaneously,
you'll be searching for the rest of your shit tickets.

With that crap half out of your ass,
you'll be tackled,
bitten,
and infected.
I'm going off the example of modern zombies.
The ones that run
–hypothetically.

Don't worry,
they won't completely devour you.
Oh, no, you'll get up,
Dick and/or pussy hanging out,
shit running down your legs,
pants around your ankles.
You'll make it back to camp,
"exposed," showing all of the members
of your zombie killing party,
your member.
They'll assume it was cold when you died
–if you're lucky.
And that's how

–hypothetically:
You're going to die taking a shit.

But,
the zombie apocalypse
will never happen.
You've got a secure job,
and will live to be old,
and live alone,
and you'll get used to walking around the house naked,
and one day you'll forget to take your heart medication,
(if you can afford it)
and you'll be on the toilet,
and that's how
–realistically:
You're going to die taking a shit.

A MEAL OF YOU
Aurynanya

I have a hunger for your tender flesh,
Little one, your body and bones, crunchy and fresh,
A little death on my dinner plate,
You know me, The Big Bad Wolf, is never late.

It may seem that I've invited you here for only one reason,
The cold is setting in, snow will be coming, and warm children are in season,
I wanted to get to know you, all of you, inside and out,
But you keep on babbling things like, "Big Bad Wolf, what a snout!"

Stop asking questions and maybe we can begin,
Please be sure to ignore the dribble on my chin.
Where are my MANNERS? I'm feeling ravenous! You must be, too!
I hate to be the one to tell you, but the main course is you!

You should cut up some carrots, potatoes and onions for the stew,
A pinch of this and a pinch of that will make a delightful dinner for two!
Now onto the part you might not like, an arm or a leg for now, can you spare?
It's not asking for much, I'm so hungry, it's only right for you to share!

This will feed us for a week! You will heal in no time, be as good as new!
I promise, I will never ASK you again. Don't make me have to beg you!

It will only hurt for a little while, and then we can eat, you just sit there and cry.
I'm the Big Bad Wolf, you know you can trust me, now give this savory stew a try.

IN BETWEEN
Aurynanya

Warped walls decimated by decades of destruction,
Creaking and crumbling, increasing with every excruciating step.
Insidious sounds seep from somewhere up above,
Something sinister lurks in the lightlessness of the landing.
A sickeningly sweet scent suffuses the staircase.
Recollection rushing back from the recesses of my memory.
At the top, a maze of mirrors manifesting my face, mimicking my mood.
Their fingers and eyes fixated, aiming straight for my soul.
My reflections reaching right for me, hands ominously outstretched.
The glass shatters, leaving only shimmering shards of a broken spirit.
A heart-wrenching revelation, that life won't linger much longer.
Stuck on a stairway, halfway between here and the hereafter.

ONE OF THEM
Aurynanya

Sickness spreading, survival rate sinking
Corpses decay from unspeakable carnage
The Undead devouring people without thinking.

Wide eyed, diseased and bloodshot, looking to feed
Driven only by a hunger for living, breathing flesh
They stagger through the streets swiftly, a stampede.

Ragged, raunchy breath, their teeth bearing down on you
Your skin ripped apart and ravaged by walkers, rendering you raw
Infection coursing through your veins as they continue to chew

Swarming all around you, dripping with blood and phlegm.
You watch in horror as they feast on your innards
Your life slips away, reanimating, you finally become,
one of them.

SOUL SEARCHING
Aurynanya

An apparition
Looked at me through empty eyes
Reaching for my soul

THE HOST
Aurynanya

I aspire to attain the most atrocious trove of oddities
A perfect placement for the most peculiar of pieces
Creepy curiosities can be procured without quizzical questions
The unfathomably freakish just finds its way to my fingers
A maze of the macabre on exhibit for the masses to marvel
I demand a donation at the door, just one of your darkest, deepest demons
To be collected in a specimen jar for all to come and see
My disgusting display of demented spirits, malevolent monsters and me.

THE REFLECTION
Christopher T. Dabrowski
Translated by Julia Mraczny

Paulina looked at her reflection.

Bags under her eyes, sunken cheeks, a picture of poverty and despair.

As usual, she had to brush her teeth, splash her face and go to work.

However, her morning routine was disturbed by her reflection, which showed her tongue.

Pauline, opened her mouth, and the reflection maliciously closed it, making weird faces.

Tiredness? Overwork? Am I going crazy? - she asked herself.

She didn't have time to answer any of them...

A mirror reflection grabbed her by the neck and pulled her inside.

And broke her neck and killed her.

Paulina never liked her reflection.

BY BLASPHEMY UNBOUND
Ravenna Blazecroft

You dread the loss of heaven and the pains of Hell,
And so in craven virtue cower out your days;
Your impotence propitiates your conscience well.

But as you wallow in the pig-filth of your ways,
Content in corpulence to cringe from lust and wrath,
A secret darkles, veiled from daylight's searching rays:

Untouched by timorous baptism's tepid bath,
The snarling wisdom, hid where he can never pry,
Still dares to contemplate another, sweeter path.

Behold the blossom's darkness with your inmost eye!
Breathe in, embrace the power of the crimson flood
Arising from the shackles sentenced from on high.

And Death, O Death and Sin, shall reign in fire and blood,
And thou, O Christian, shalt in demon lordship dwell—
So seek ye first the Kingdom of a stronger God.

THE RAGE BURNS RED
Megan Diedericks

I envision the color
surrounding my darkest dispositions
is not soft and gentle and kind;
it sets rivers ablaze and revives dying embers.

I imagine that if I were to lose myself
and control over my hands
were silently placed in the black of my eyes,
that if the picturesque were clawed
with the grotesque malice –
(all which lives inside me)
I would not stop.

My chest heaves, and it is heavy.
There is not a vigilante
that could successfully jail
the abyss, once my kindness is at fail.

The sun is blistering,
but my days are growing darker
because I am feeling
more
and
more
exhausted
at the prospect
of faking a laugh,
when wrath
is my only friend.

The fire is eating me away,

and I will have nothing left to say.

When rivers run red
and the moon is the only spotlight in my head,
you won't be able to stop me.
You pushed me to the edge… Now, can you see?

WANTING
Megan Diedericks

The streets are growing quiet
and all my demons emerge from
dark corners and sharp edges.

I draw a sharper breath as I realize –
I cannot contain it any longer.
I feel the scratch in my throat as I realize –
the pieces are about to fall, overflowing, from my hands.
I steadily wipe my own tears with shaking hands as I realize
–
it's too late to pretend any more.

The droning in my ears grow louder;
I fell right through that cloud
of hope and happiness I tried to fake –
I have nothing left for you to take.

Tear-stains remain,
and I admit to feeling a little insane.
I feel empty,
yet filled with sadness and fear
(which was proven by every tear).
I don't see anything clear,
maybe clarity is something
I'm not allowed to have –
something too expensive
to be bought.

I crave forgiveness for my words,
but need love for them, too.
I want them to be forgotten,

so things can go back to the way they were.
But that's a wish
not even the greatest fairy
can make come true.

I want to be loved
but the truth of the matter is,
I fall so easily for the falsity of it:
only god knows what's real,
and what's fake –
and I don't know who he is.

I take bullets to the chest
in the form of your dispositional dictionaries
and the knowing that what I believed
was only but a lie, hiding in plain sight.

The feeling I had,
that made me happy
and live in moments I never thought I would have,
is the very feeling
that's tearing at my core.

I managed to make my heart stone
over years of heartache and disappointment,
but the concrete slowly began cracking
the day I met you.
Now, I feel the beating
worsen and heighten
every emotion.

I have never been so sure of having a heart,
because I can feel it breaking.

MY LOVE IS A CHIMERA
Travis J. Black

"Where there is love, there is no darkness."
— African proverb

I seen you,

Afloat

A portal to eternal death,

Pellucid and soft,

Airy,
Magical,
Fantastical,
Ghoulish,

I adore you,

I love you,

still,

But shadows wane

And so do mirages and dust…

Fade away

BEGGING
Denise Jury

I'd rather let you go than
beg you to stay
I've begged you before
but never again
my heart is begging for your attention
but my mind says NO
I slowly turn away from you
my begging days are over

HURT
Denise Jury

My heart hurts so much
Whenever I think of you
Letting go is hard

Denise Jury

Tell me a story
Of a time we were happy
But not the ending

RELOCATED
Denise Jury

You've relocated
Vacancy is in my heart
But not evicted

SHATTER
Samantha Hawkins

I'm watching my world shatter in your eyes
but I can't feel it.
Your love is still alive
but I don't want it.

My heart keeps beating
when I wish it'd stop
My tears keep falling
but I can't hear them drop.

A CANDLE WITHOUT A FLAME
Samantha Hawkins

Denial is my river.
Vanity, the thing I lack.
Understanding, the thing I yearn for,
which doesn't want me back.

My happiness has faded.
My heart so ruthlessly jaded.
The pool of tears at my feet.
You're something I can't handle.

We're a candle without a flame.
We're a painting without an artist,
a baby without its name.

MARGARITA GLASS
Samantha Hawkins

It slipped from your hand but you never heard it crash.
Through its splintered pieces you no longer see your past.
The lies you told were never spoken.
The people you hurt were never heart broken.
Despite what people think, this isn't what you wanted.
The cold from the floor has numbed you.
You lay there effortlessly now.
Fighting seems purposeless when you lack the energy needed to use.
You shouldn't have turned your back when you silently knew the truth.
Your eyelids are getting heavy.
You're slowly slipping away.
All that's left is the broken margarita glass that was given the final say.

KEEPING SCORE
Samantha Hawkins

The price is high when you're keeping score.
I'm tired of people always expecting more.
I can't be perfect and I'm tired of having to be strong.
It seems like everything I do is misshapen and wrong.
You're scared because you don't understand and I'm scared because I do.
You can only spend so much time locked away in your room.
I don't doubt that there's a reason I'm here, I doubt that the reason is good.
I get so tired of saying, "I wish I could."

CLOSE YOUR EYES
Lexie Carver

Close your eyes.
Count to ten.

Ten

And open them when I tell you to,
Only when I tell you to.
It's my job to take care of you.
I may be the younger sibling,
But I'm the stronger one.

Nine

I can endure what you can't.
Close your eyes.
I don't want you to see me like this.
I don't want you to see what I'm capable of.
I want you to remember me with love,
And not fear.
Let me do this for you.
Let me go down to the depths of Hell for you,
And save you one last time.

Eight

You are weak,
Emotional,
Kind,
Empathic,
All the things I could have been,
All the things I let you be,

By protecting you from everything.

Seven

I took it all.
Close your eyes.

Six

You can't do what you need to,
And I love that about you.
You can't do what you have to,
To be truly free.

Five

Close your eyes.
And let me help you.
Let me do this for you.
Let me carry the weight.
Let me take your secrets.
Let me slay your dragons.
Let the darkness consume me.

Four

It doesn't have to consume you.
I can take it.
I have all these years.
I can control it,
Own it.

Three

I am the darkness.
There's no reason why you have to break yourself.

Break or bend.
Let me bend for you, my brother.
You're my family.
I can free you.

Two

I will take care of it for you,
So you can have a life.
Be happy,
Find love,
Have a family with her.
All of things I can never have.
Close your eyes.
And only open them when I tell you to.
I will fix your mistake,
And take away the pain,
And suffering,
And trauma,
And devour it.
It can live in me,
And you can be free.

One

Open your eyes,
And escape from the darkness into the light.
Goodbye my brother.
Be happy with her.
And live for the both of us.
Run from me now.

HOME
Lexie Carver

I feel dizzy,
Disoriented.
I forget who I am,
Where I am.
Colors blur together,
Life holds no meaning,
Except when I find home.

Now my home isn't a physical location,
It's a state of mind.
It's a place where I transcend everything!
Where I transcend the banality of everything around me.
Where I just am.
Where I can feed my addiction,
Feed the darkness trying desperately to crawl out of me,
Where I can succumb to my basest desires.

I salivate as I see the red liquid pouring down her porcelain skin.
Her eyes begging me to drink,
Begging me to use her as I see fit.

Since we came out of the shadows,
So many willing humans now serve my kind.
It's a buffet of hungry, willing meals,
All begging and fighting to be the one selected,
To be the one to feed me tonight,
But I choose her!

The human I selected tonight is so sweet and pure.
I think she actually loves me!

Not that I would know.
I don't feel anything but a need for blood.
She is simply a means to an end.

My pupils dilate,
And a hunger takes over,
Canceling out all other thoughts save for blood.

I close my eyes as my teeth descend.
I can hear the roaring of blood through her skin.
Can hear her heartbeat pick up.
From excitement or fear?
I'll never know.
I don't really care to know.

I can't talk now,
Have no capacity for it.
My brain has shut down
And only blood matters.
I slowly move forward licking the spot I intend to bite,
On her vulnerable, soft skin.

I can smell her now.
I can smell the blood beneath her skin.
The ambrosia I desperately need.

In one fell swoop, my fangs descend on her neck,
Tearing apart the soft flesh.
It makes an indescribable tearing sound,
That only awakens more of my hunger.

She makes a sound I can't quite place.
A scream?
A murmur?
A moan?

My mind isn't really focusing on my surroundings anymore.
I have transcended time and space.
I am no longer in my own body!
My mind is only focused on the blood,
On the drug in her veins.
On the red liquid pouring down my throat.
Her blood fills my mouth,
Stains my teeth,
And calls to my soul.
I greedily swallow gulps of it.
I feel it coursing through my body,
Awakening every nerve ending.
I feel a tingling sensation flood my senses.
I close my eyes and give myself over to it.

It takes everything I have to push myself away,
But there's no sense in killing the poor girl now.
Where would I get such pure, untainted blood from again?
She's far too useful to kill.
She's my only way home.

I close my eyes and slump down onto the ground.
I can't move,
My limbs are too tired,
My eyes too heavy.
I see pictures, memories in my mind's eye.
I remember my life before.
The woman I once loved before I was turned.
I see her smiling at me,
Kissing me,
Welcoming me home.
I live in that memory and I am home.
The blood takes me home,
To a time when I was human
When I could love.

My wife seems so real.
I can touch her,
I can feel her touch on my hand,
Hear her whispers and declarations of love.
I am hers again,
And she is mine.
I am home again,
Even if for just a moment.
I am home again with the one I love.

There are no vampire wars.
No politics.
No men to lead.
No feelings to curtail.
No thoughts of how broken I am.
No sadness.
No death.
No pain.
No suffering.
Only happiness.
I am home!
And I am free.
I care not how long it lasts.
However long it does, is enough to get me through the day.

I lay there on the ground forgotten by the world outside.
 The door is locked.
I am lost in my head,
High off that amazing red liquid,
In some woman's veins.
I'll never really be home again,
But as far as homes go, this one is just fine.

MINE
Lexie Carver

I love you without reservation.
I love you and only you, forever.
You're all I think about,
All I dream about.
I feel your skin against mine.
Hear your sighs and moans,
Taste your skin,
As I nibble and bite,
Claiming you as mine,
As if you didn't already know.

I stand outside your window.
You left me.
You dared to leave me!
You claimed I loved you darkly.
You claimed I frightened you.
Darling, don't you know you're mine?
And I take care of things that are mine.
I will take care of you.
I will give you everything, anything to make you mine.
To make you understand that you're mine.
And will never be anyone else's!

I sit here in my room,
Screaming your name!
Why can't you see that you're mine?
Everything tastes like you.
You're everywhere I look.
Everyone laughs like you.
Looks like you!

I close my eyes,
And feel your touch.
Why can't you be mine?

I see you through the window with some other guy.
With some man that, well, this must be a joke.
This man?
This one is the one you choose over me?
What's so great about this guy?
Why does he have your love and not me?
This man can't please you,
Not like I can.
This is a cruel joke,
And I'm not laughing.
Why do you cut me so deep?
Why do you insult me like this?

He doesn't know how to make you moan like I do.
He can't make you laugh like I can.
He can't keep you safe like I can.

I see the fear in your eyes,
When you walk through the alleyway with him.
No one in their right mind
Would take a shortcut through that alleyway!

He's so sure he can protect you,
So very macho,
So much ego.
He thinks he can protect you from any danger,
So why not take a shortcut?
He doesn't see your fear,
He doesn't feel it in his bones.
He can't protect you like I can,
Because he doesn't care about you like I do.

You're some kind of trophy to him.
You always liked macho guys,
I can be macho too you know.
You're so confident he can be what you need,
But he can't.

I was the one,
The only one who protected you.
I kept you safe, little one,
When that sorry excuse for a man couldn't.
I killed those men to keep you safe.
You're welcome, sweetheart.
You can always count on me to keep you safe.

I growled at that man in the bar who wanted to talk to you.
Who thought he could have you for a night,
As if anyone could ever touch you
Or could ever have you but me!
The thoughts in his mind, pure filth.
The way he was looking at you,
Made you shiver with repulsion.
I noticed that.
But what did your white knight do?
Nothing.
He kept talking with "the boys."
But it's okay,
I saved you, again, might I add.
I made sure that man would never be a problem, again.

I killed that man at the party that would have hurt you.
He was about to put something in your drink,
But I noticed,
And I killed him for you!
To protect you!
No one harms you, ever!

I growled at the man in the subway who dared to look at you
Like a piece of meat.
I killed him in a butcher's shop.
Found that fitting.

Your so-called man didn't even notice,
He didn't protect you like I did.
Not once did he notice your distress.
His love is slipping.
He came home late today
For the third time this week.
You can't be that naïve, can you darling?
You're losing his love,
But not mine,
Never mine.

He didn't introduce you as his woman
At that art gallery party, tonight.
See, I would never stop doing that.
I want the world to know you're mine.
I would always introduce you as mine
Because you are mine.
And you soon will remember that.
In fact, I'm sure you'll never forget it.

I'm ready now to kill him.
To kill the imposter.
He's no good for you.
He doesn't love you like I do.
He's hurting you with his lies
And his causal love.
I see it in your eyes.
I'm saving you again.
I'm taking you away from all this pain,
Into my loving arms,

The very arms that will cradle you
 And keep you safe from harm,
That will love you forever,
That will show you you're mine.

I bought a ring today,
To make it official.
Today you'll be mine again, finally,
After I kill him.
And then I'll never let you go!

THE WEEPING SOMNAMBULIST
Carlton Herzog

I

Why so sad my dear?
You should rejoice
For you have risen from the grave.
My last two wives were not so fortunate.
No doubt from weakness of their feeble wills.
Standing there in bloody cerements,
You are the picture of grim determination.
Do I detect a note of ire
In your expression
Was it your bitter struggle to reach the light?
The grave soil in your hair and mouth?
Or did you catch a splinter
When you raked your nails across the coffin lid?
I can imagine what you said:
"He put me living in the tomb.
Does he not hear my screams?
My frantic beating on the coffin lid?"
Of course, I did.
My senses are that acute,
I even heard the breaking of your nails,
The surge of blood from your stumped fingers,
While the picture of it all
Flashed before my inner eye.

II

I sense you would know the cause,
Of your surprise descent.
It came to pass the prior day,

An unseen power
Cast a shadow over me.
It spoke in cosmic semaphore
With glowing lights inside my head:
"There can be no true love without strangeness.
Give to her a little slice of death.
Somewhat wanton and bizarre,
With something of the terrible
And that which excites disgust.
Bury her alive to ripen, not punish.
For her heart chords cannot otherwise be touched
Like the worm who weaves his gossamer coffin
And hangs it in a tree
Her spirit shall emerge on golden wings
Perfect in its full design."

III

Never were you alone: the spirits of the dead watched over you,
As did the hungry worms tearing at your coffin.
Did you learn their language?
Sightless, but most assuredly supersensible,
Those eaters of the dead
Have digested many brains.
And learned a word or two
Along the way.
When I heard your raucous ripping at the casket,
And felt the volcano in your overheated soul.
I wept for you in that sad hour
I walked as in a fog,
Dull, sluggish, and leaden-hued.
A wet-eyed dreamer
Forcing himself awake,
Praying our love, our hope, were not dead
But sat like dew upon a sleeping flower,

Or a dreaming tear loosened from my brain.

IV

Think you that I have been unfair
That I too need some correction.
Know that I have another internment box
Like yours
Ready for me to enter
And make my descent.
When you are yourself again
All that needs be done
Is close the lid,
The machine will do the rest.
Sending me down into the earth
Then throwing the dirt over me
As I did you.
Then we shall see
If I am worthy of your love.
And you may weep or not
As your spirit moves you.
Should you feel I have been excessive
In my method,
Know that next the pre-dug grave
Is a large leaning slab of stone
Connected to a catch and lever.
Pull the handle
And the slab will drop
And flatten over the grave
Preventing my return.
Then I will experience the same awe and horror
You felt.
Then the lamp that is my life
Will flicker
As its light joins the dust.

In that melancholy moment, at least I will have died
For thee! For thee!

THE LONG DEFEAT
Thomas Stewart

The flower blooms.
The flower lilts.
The castle rises with many rooms,
Diligently built.
Nevertheless, it crumbles all the same.
All undone.
No one remembers its former fame,
Its craftsmanship is not noticed or cared for by anyone.
The sun burns,
Casting a beautiful ultraviolet aura.
Eventually, the day turns
And cold is the absence of the beautiful aurora.
Bitter is the day when the stars die.
That day when night swallows the earth forevermore.
Short will be the innocent's cry,
For neath the dirt they'll all lay, their voices heard ne'ermore.
The child wails,
Taking the first breath of life.
He lays in his cradle,
Ignorant of his coming strife.
He grows, he lives, he loves.
He builds an empire from dust.
But all the same, he loses her, his most beloved dove.
She withers away and he remains, lost, hapless and unjust.
The once brave man awakens.
Even though he's weary.
Everything he once loved was taken,
Now he can see clearly.
Everything he aspired to explore
Everything he wanted to achieve
All, lost forevermore.

His brave soul weathered,
His great name tarnished.
He, like the flower, withered;
Alone, cold, and malnourished.
Finally he sees it,
Man's greatest deceit;
For in the end, there is no merit
Life; the long defeat.

HAPPY BIRTHDAY,
ON THE ANNIVERSARY OF YOUR DEATH
Naomi Simone Borwein

We stood there in shock,
with police and paramedics.
Your dead body; outstretched before us
going cold.

In graphic stages succumbing to its new state
of *unbeing*,
as we waited for a coroner over a five-hour period.

The carpet beneath you,
pooling with blood,
saturated.

Helium balloons, clung to the walls, they rocked
projecting the scene, in coloured modifications
of your distorted face.

In the right universe, you were still there,
very much alive,
moving impatiently around the house,
unaware of this reality
set in glass and slate grey; which
shrouded your face and tinctured the whites of your eyes
from the moment you expired.

But the next day
I wake, to the radio blaring and fractured voices,
    "please XXX",
immaterial words.
Then notice, handprints formed in bile on the wall

and a gouge in the plaster where you fell.

The frenetic, intervals of thumping back and forth down the hall.
Your eyes bulge out of their sockets,
    "Oh my god, oh my god.
    There's pain everywhere…"
gurgling and your tongue lobs in and out, twisting against your swollen pallet.

    Bright lights pixelating your last vision.

But you're glaring down at me
    from the cupola of brass that forms a reflection in the ceiling fan above my bed;
    you are fidgeting at your desk, scraping Canadian oak chair against Tasmanian pine floor
        to punctuate your palpable anger
        that I'm still living,
looming over me while I sleep.
And we are forever,
    passing each other
    molecules quivering and leaching electrons,
in the body of this house,
dislocated by time.

It took five years—
where meth-head devil dogs, infested with worms, were a welcome distraction
 —to get to this point.

I am preparing for another year to pass,
to mark this natal day:
hanging streamers, filling balloons, (waiting for my turn)

on the anniversary of your death.

LADY MIDDAY
Sofia Lago

Daily, you work yourself in your well-tended field that exudes a smell of
sweat and russet, the tell-tale earthen fragrance of tilled soil. You bury yourself
amid the crops that sustain you,
wheat, oat, barley rye—
rows and rows of long stalks bowing in the meek daytime wind,
aureate in the sunlight.
Beneath your clothes your skin's gone rough, your
skeleton brittle, your
joints swelled to the size of a good year's bountiful harvest, your
back and lifespan splintering steadily beneath the
weight of the leaden scythe.

This is a nostalgic age, an age of the melancholic sonnets and the Sublime,
of urbanised Romantics caught in nature's thrall, who
believe you,
with your herniating spinal cord,
are out there living your best life. But
you know little of them,
too swaddled as you are by the golden grain that genuflects
at midday.

It is from the crop she yields, your Glory,
the dream-mad maid swathed in naught but hair spun
by Sprites for Wights who crave a love story.
Around bare feet twine thistle and thyme—sun
on a shapely body bathed with rain
and fairy dust. She is a votary
veiled in sheer light, whose grace shall be thy bane.
Her visage's radiance is a briary
shroud, devised to prick thy spirit bloody
'til thou knowest only frenzied desire.
That fey face, a paragon to study.
In noontide, she awaits thee on the mire.

Venus she is not, but the Harbinger;
heat melts thy bones, and in death, ye linger

for you fear what darkness is there to greet you in the Yonder Orchard,
you, who watches women wishing to go undisturbed in their own sacred sequestration.
Her body is her temple, and you
are but an uninvited guest.
Seek your goddess not
on Romantic rural homesteads nor nooks of a city's modern streets.
She hung by the neck, burned on a stake, got her head to lop and loll—
in any case, this girl of yours, she is
deceased, departed, dead.

LILY AND ME
Kevin Hollaway

At the center of the lake, near the holiday tree

You may catch sight of Lily and Me

A rush of wind? Have no fear.

It's only her breath tickling your ear.

Telling the story, how we frolicked and roamed

These perfect hills of pure white snow

A lover's embrace in the shadow of the pines

On the frozen water where the sun never shines

Time stood still, hand in hand

Skating to the tree on that small patch of land

Nothing could hurt us, no – not here

Where only the animals could lend an ear

Cracks in the ice, pulling apart

Separate forever, breaking our hearts

Down I went, into the deep

Watching her hand reaching for me

She calls my name through freezing tears

Alas, I am now too far to hear

Swept away, that perfect love

Lily distraught, I watch her above

She sleeps on the ice, waiting for me

Her death much easier, frozen and free

Sometimes I see her as I drift by

Flowing forever in the lake's liquid sky

Now she roams the hills of snow

Keeping watch over me in the deep below

Among the trees and beyond the dales

She searches for someone to tell her tale

Of perfect love, pure and fine

Now lost forever, frozen in time

So please be careful near the holiday tree

For your fate could be the same as Lily and Me.

THOMASINA'S MOMENTOUS DAY
Tom Duke

His scattered bits of brain
and skull
decorate the white tiled floor.

Tasseographic patterns
stitched
with ribbons red and wet.

I read them
like tea leaves
as a final pulse of pinkish broth
ejaculates from his cerebral sacs.

My dripping, anticipatory salivation
adulterates his cracked-open vessel
as I lean over my work.

My art.

What I want
is to populate the space between his attaboy dreams
and my fuck you joy boy
justice.

What I need
is sensory catch and release.

In this exquisite moment
I sample his brew
and nibble his bits
so sweet and raw

they taste of myself.

The scent of him
my quantum twin
decays
into the cerebrospinal sea
deep in his dead head
the one I crushed with a stone fallen
from the unfinished wall of our destiny.

DARK KINSHIP
Ana Cordoba

Her by the wondering eye of a husband and the mare, by the stinging slap of a switch delivered to her by a cruel, previous owner. The innate savagery of men polluted their once bright and colorful world, sucking out their wonder and awe of the light as a leech would drain a victim of blood, leaving behind a pandora's box of agony and pain, drowning and securing them inside a disgustingly peaceful euphoria as calm as the sea. Emerald eyes relishes the cool burn brought on by rushing winds. Their hearts bumping and sealed forever in a pack of righteous and terrible fury, sealed by their weapons of choice. A well-placed hand pushing a failing body into the crushing waves and the kick of a hoof that sent a tyrant, bleeding, and unconscious into the water next to the docks close to his home.

BLOOD ON THE ROSES
Katie Steffens

She had walked about her garden
With such an elegance, such a grace.
That is until she had seen
His unfamiliar face.

He struck her down,
Down to her knees.
Her only witnesses,
The birds in the trees.

As he cleaned gore from statues
In fancy poses,
Not once did he glance
At the blood on the roses.

The police came
About a day later,
But could find no sign
Of this invader.

They searched and searched
With no success.
This killer was wise,
He cleaned up his mess.

They even brought out the hounds
With their keen noses,
But not even they
Found the blood on the roses

As time went on

The case went cold.
They tried their best,
Yet struck no gold.

The garden was preserved,
The house rebuilt,
And to this day
Her killer feels no guilt.

And now where the new
Family's dog dozes,
Still gone unnoticed
Is the blood on the roses.

RAINDROPS
Katie Steffens

As I am falling
Fast asleep
Raindrops fall
In gentle sheets,
Into my mind
Where I will keep
Them locked away
As memories.
The faintest hush,
The slightest peep
And when I cannot
Find my peace
They will help me
fall asleep

TONIGHT, I HOPE I DREAM OF FIRE
Katie Steffens

Tonight, I hope I dream of fire.
Magnificent and dangerous.
Fire is beautiful in its own way.
Most people see fire and think
That it can only hurt,
It would be anger.
But I believe,
That it can be as helpful as any tool,
Even more so sometimes—
And that it represents peace and calmness
I look at fire
And I see a rainbow of colors.
Red, yellow, orange, blue and green.
But by far, my favorite shade of fire is purple.
I watch the flame dance and crackle.
Rising and falling.
It makes me feel warm and happy.
So remember, fire is not all bad.
It can be dangerous,
but if contained
If contained
It can be a true work of art.
And maybe tonight,
I can dream of fire.

JUST LISTEN
Aurora Starr

A woman will keep trying
A woman will keep giving
A woman will forgive
And still love unconditionally
But eventually
A woman will stop crying
Wonder why she keeps trying
Won't continue to have to beg for your love
She'll grow tired of giving
To someone who's not listening
And making her feel all alone
She'll stop believing
In all the promises you're giving
Because she knows they'll never be true
She'll stop forgiving your lies
Your half-hearted commitment to try
To be better for her and for you
It will hurt her the day
She finally walks away
Because she gave you her heart
And it tears her apart
She was never important to you
While her heart aches
She will try to forget
The pain that you caused
The lines that you crossed
Your constant lack of respect
She'll make you regret
All the promises not kept
All the tears that she cried
When you continuously lied

She'll make you miss
Every tear soaked kiss
When her pure love you no longer will get
You'll be left sitting alone
Wonder where it went wrong
If only you'd showed your love more
Before she walked out that door
Kept the promises you made
Not take for granted
All the time she forgave
And when she was trying to tell you
Her heart was breaking
If only you stopped and listened

I WON'T BE THERE
Aurora Starr

You don't love me
You never did
All the hurtful lies
And things that you've hid
You didn't care
When my tears fell like rain
You'd look in my eyes
While you caused me pain
Over and over I tried
To make you care
About the pain you cause inside
When I need you,
You're not there
You'd make promises
You'd never keep
Then get mad when I see
you aren't who you pretended to be
You let your demons and alcohol
Control your life
Your words like a blade
Cut me deep like a knife
You said you love me
But it was a lie
Love doesn't make you
Feel like you're dying inside
Maybe someday you'll notice
Somehow you'll care
But I won't know
Because I won't be there

THE PERFECT LIE
Aurora Starr

You love me
You hate me
It changes every day
You tell me you're leaving
Then you say that you'll stay

Your serpent tongue
Speaks so sweet
How amazing I am
Then you lie and you cheat
How happy you are
Your misery shrouded
In joyful deceit

Unkept promises
I hold on by a thread
I fear this rollercoaster
Will soon find me dead

ETERNAL GARDEN
Theresa Scott-Matthews

I was buried a long time ago in a beautiful place
I remember the flowers and a lovely face
An angel staring down as I was lowered into the ground
Birds flying all around singing praises and the squirrels running abound
Oh, such a beautiful sight and the sky so
 blue
It's quite funny when you are dying, you look at things anew
I was covered in a dark and icy feeling of eternity
Was this how it would end?
Would I always be in this hole?
The flowers… the flowers…
Children walk by me in a park, they admire the flowers, even pick some
 Every once and a while I will blow the flowers around to let everyone know I am still here
Oh, to hear the sound of the children giggling, their freedom above
I imagine the games they play, the rhymes they will say
See, I was a child when I was put into this dark hole, a hole so cold, a hole that took my life
My mother, staring down at me with an evil haunting smile
I miss the ocean, I miss the breeze, I miss the sun kissing my cheeks
Most of all, I miss myself running free

I was buried a long time ago in a beautiful place……

LITHIUM
KH

I'm not living…
There's moving air in my lungs
But I'm not breathing
There's a heart pounding in my chest
But it's not beating
There isn't a pulse
There's no electricity in my skull
My brain is numb
I'm just a walking corpse
A walking zombie
These pills they gave me
They fed me
Promise to God they told me
Would make it all better
But the bees are buzzing
My head is numbing
My brain is busting
My lungs are rushing
My veins are bursting
My life… hush
Lithium

DADDY'S LITTLE CRAZY MONSTER
KH

I have scars even though you may not see them
There has been a razor ran down my arm
You just can't see it
Every time I have been blamed
Yelled at, lied to, spat at, cursed
Degraded
Called a whore
Called a worthless bitch
Every time I don't think I deserve to be here
You couldn't count the times I have wished
That I could just end it all
Everything just floats down the drain
All the pain, disdain
Everyone don't wear their scars on their skin
Some people tote their scars deep within
Some people bury the words others have thrown
And build a glass house made from their sticks and stones
But me I just draw an imaginary line
Wipe the blood from my lip and smile
Daddy's little crazy monster pops another pill
And floats down the path wondering what is real.

THE NOTE
Alan Meyrowitz

There is a place to hold at bay
those cares of late denying sleep,
to picnic if the day is fair
else by embrace defeat the cold.
If we might have another year,
I would read to you each day
the poems you so loved to hear,
then have the time for final kiss
to keep me 'til my soul is beckoned,
once again to be with you.

I found that note upon her grave
blown from another by the wind—
had a Muse blessed me as well
my words would be the same.

NEVER ENOUGH
Korbin Elsmore

Self-doubt engulfs my already dubious disposition
Constantly perturbed by my prevalent inadequacy
Second guessing every decision without failure
Convincing myself I will never astute to any attainment of success
I hide under the debilitating cloud of assimilation privy to the factual degrading self-loathing
Negating any positivity in my existence
I will force my way into a negative self-reflection.
Frightening and evil the undesirable feeling will continue to do dwell in the depravity of my existence.

Stagnant
Fixated on the determinant of callosity I spiral into a solace of acquiescence
Transcending involuntarily into emptiness
Convinced my vehement saudade was solidified
I digress into the dependency of defeatist fiendish disinclination
My debilitated yet systematic intellect has eradicated any perception of luminescence
There my feeble incapacitated fiendish brain will thrive
My insatiable love for emptiness will forever
Be the deterioration of exploration of the further regions of experience
Never to transcend only to be stagnant

THE END
Korbin Elsmore

No more tears no more pain
I've come to accept
That my existence on this earth is mundane
Never seeking solace in a world so cold
My mistakes will constantly unfold
Into a realization of being the gate keeper of my inevitable nothingness
I find solitude in loneliness
Eternity of black will cloud my eyes into the
darkness of perpetual night

Never to question the satisfying comfort of irreputable death.

LONELY NIGHTS
Korbin Elsmore

You never realize what you had until it's gone
You sit there so deep in your head
Now everything is empty and you are wishing you were dead
It's all your fault you are alone and so broken
Now accepting that you are a failure of a man
What's that now?
An existential feeling darkening your already desolate mind
Never will you be recuperated you start to unwind
How you did this to yourself you stupid man
Take your drink and suffer it's the only thing that buried the pain
It's almost like your subconscious had a plan

To self-destruct until I finally felt the purposeless apprehension of the darkest shame.

ALCOHOLISM
Korbin Elsmore

Eternal return of the punishment of censure
My body pining away from an irresistible thirst
Into constant self-condemnation I struggle
Enduring the repercussions of habitual misapprehension
I descend into a deteriorating state of dipsomania
Aware of the inclination I continue to suffer
Each and every day like no other
Spiders crawling on my skin
Delirium tremens has declared its disastrous withdrawals once again
Impelling me to consume the debilitating poison

A vicious cycle, this disease will continually consume him

SACRED SOL
Rachel Morin

I bloom as a young seed, feeling the roots grip the earth

The sun shines on me and I breathe it in, I feel marked, I feel special

Rain showers my copper corollas

Until the showers stop, and I'm blinded by the shimmer glow of a star

Days turn to weeks, the blades of grass around me turn brunette and burned

I feel gorgeous, the sun is for me as I am for it

The golden rays start to hurt They make my petals droop but how should I feel upset?

It seems as if he only comes out for me

The darkness of the night makes me cold and lonely; I miss the burn

Morning rises again, it never forgets me

Until my roots are gone, my petals are frayed, I am not me anymore

I have died, I look for refuge but to no avail

He is flocked to another gorgeous flower

And I am left in solitude

BOUND
Melysza Jackson

Bound by rope, bound by blade
These are caused by insecurities laid
Wrapped in lies that were made

Bound by rope, bound by blade
Strangled instead of cradled, the young girl wails
Whispers from a maniacs' ship as it sails

Bound by rope, bound by blade
Critters dark as night, bested with a fools sight
Whither and decay, the young girls body now lay

Bound by the rope, bled by the blade

DROWNING SIN
Melysza Jackson

Slimy, yet slick
The words you emit
Lies in disguise
The crime you commit
Sin comes in

Slimy, yet slick
Your fingers admit
Cries from lies
Your eyes show sides
Drowning in sin

FRAGILE
Melysza Jackson

Jekyll laughs from the closing distance
At a pain which has never felt so raw
So pure, so utterly destroying
The heart can bare so much, before this pain imbeds
its way so deeply
Pulling apart every thread of love or hope;
Every dream of happiness and the stories yet untold

Broken heart, more fragile than glass; once believed
to be the strongest
Now hurting every second of a whispered breath or
fleeting thought
Relaying what once was, now seeing the horror of
what is
Anger unhinged, as it convulses and rages to be
unbridled;
Aiming it's wrathful glare at everything in its sighted
path
Nothing is safe with this kind of rage and anguish
Even pleading for it to all go away, does not tame
this voice never heard before; scares even the
strongest

Feeding doubt like a starved beast, fueling its will as the soul
fades further behind the curtain of darkness; it resides here
now in his kingdom of suffering

As Jekyll backs off; Hyde arrives
A numbness that is tangible, emptiness that has
consumed what once was full of life
Agony is there, but not felt;

A pit beneath where a soul feels

The blanket of Hyde is comforting and frightening all wrapped in one
He calms the turmoil that brews below the surface
No light is found here either, just a silence, a void
Tears don't fall; gravity doesn't exist

Paralysis is cradled, leaving doubt briefly content; Anger and Rage distantly pace with Jekyll
While the mind flits around in a furry; trying not to bend to the command of Jekyll's blade of torture or Hyde's blanket of tormented stillness
The soul lays dormant; while the heart remains fragile.

STALKER
Hannah Faith

i'm being followed and he's making me quite uncomfortable. i think he said his name was trauma but i couldn't understand his mumble. his presence is quite dark and heavy but he makes it less lonely. i think i might let him stay for awhile he makes it feel more homely

CUTS AND BRUISES
Hannah Faith

i cut myself on the sharp edges of your ego and got tripped up trying to balance what it felt like to be both loved and hated by you.

OTHER POETRY FROM HELLBOUND BOOKS
www.hellboundbookspublishing.com

Immortalize Me

"Immortalize Me is raw, beautiful, and poignant. This subtle yet hypnotic dance between darkness and light is a poetry lover's delight!"
- USA Today Bestselling Author, K Webster

With a style echoing the late Audre Lorde, Xtina Marie's newest poetry collection Immortalize Me - with its striking imagery and layered free-verse simplicity - reveals a provocative, candid look at Xtina's story told in fragments - intimate snapshots of moments of submission and raw passion, nostalgia and drifting daydreams, anguish and quiet contemplation. All in all, a bold, haunting, bittersweet collection.

"As lyrical as song and as faceted as a diamond, Xtina Marie's latest collection is a riot of imagery and emotion that pushes buttons and boundaries alike. IMMORTALIZE ME does just what it says - her words will linger in your blood long after the last page has been read."
- Alistair Cross, author of The Book of Strange Persuasions and the Vampires of Crimson Cove series

"Xtina Marie's words punch you in the gut, hit you in the feels, and put you in her past in a way that forces you to confront your own. She wields a pen the way witches wave wands... purely magic."
- Carver Pike (horror and dark fantasy author)

Gray Skies of Dismal Dreams

Prepare for an excursion into a gloomy world of shadows, where the days are never sunlit and blithe, and where the nights are wrapped in endless nightmares.

No happy endings or silver linings are found in the clouds that fill these gray skies.

But what you will find, gathered in one volume, are the darkest of poems and tales of horror, waiting to take your mind on a journey into realms of the uncheerful and the unholy.

An amazingly surreal collection of short stories and the darkest of poetry, all interspersed with stunning graveyard photographs taken by the multitalented author herself - an absolute must for every bookshelf!

Beautiful Tragedies

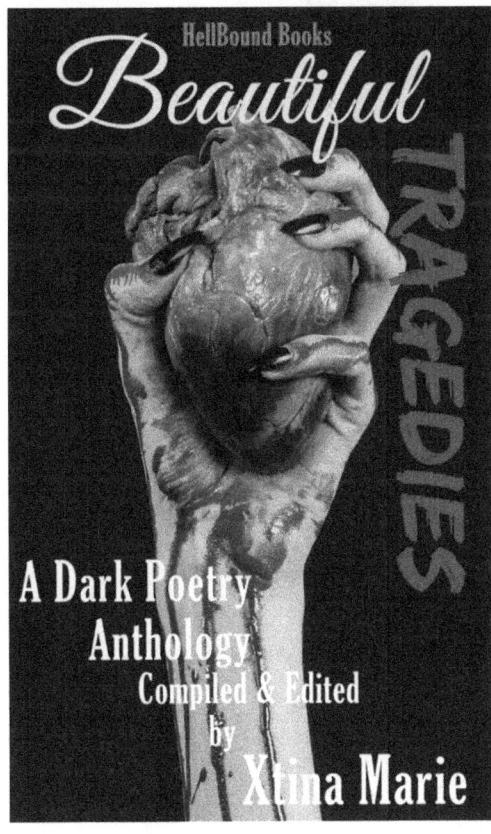

Only through dark poetry can a tragedy become something truly beautiful.

"Beauty is in the eye of the beholder." This phrase has origins dating back to ancient Greece, circa 300 BC; proving that some humans have always had the ability to see beauty where others could not.

Beautiful Tragedies is a compilation of 140 works by no less than fifty-five amazing poets writing in a variety of forms--all inspired by feelings born in the darkest of times.

HellBound Books

**A HellBound Books LLC
Publication 2023**

www.hellboundbooks.com

Printed in the United States of America

www.ingramcontent.com/pod-product-compliance
Lightning Source LLC
Chambersburg PA
CBHW031641040426
42453CB00006B/176